I0459257

the promise of His presence

A 30-DAY DEVOTIONAL JOURNAL
daily reminders that God is with you

the
promise
of His
presence

catherine mcdaugale

The Promise of His Presence

Copyright © 2025 Catherine McDaugale

www.CatherineMcDaugale.com

Published by Walk By Faith Media, LLC

Littleton, Colorado

ISBN: 978-1-956509-11-3

Unless otherwise indicated, all Scripture quotations are from the New King James Version. Copyright © 1982 by Thomas Nelson, Inc. Used by permission. All rights reserved.

Scripture quotations marked NLT are from the Holy Bible, New Living Translation. Copyright © 1996, 2004, 2007 by Tyndale House Foundation. Used by permission of Tyndale House Publishers. All rights reserved.

Any internet addresses in this book are offered as a resource. While all links are active at the time of publication, because of the dynamic nature of the internet, some web addresses or links contained in this book may have changed and may no longer be valid. They are not intended in any way to be or imply an endorsement by Walk By Faith Media, and Walk By Faith Media cannot vouch for the content of these sites for the life of this book.

All rights reserved. No part of this publication may be reproduced in any form, stored in any retrieval system, used by AI learning models, or transmitted in any form by any means—electronic, mechanical, photocopy, recording, or otherwise—without the prior permission of the publisher, except as provided by United States of America copyright law and fair use.

Cover design: Matt McDaugale

Author photo: Aaron Lucy

Printed in the United States of America

For Jesus:
Thank You for Your presence in my life.

Let us hold fast the confession of our hope without wavering, for He who promised is faithful.

— HEBREWS 10:23

Day 1

> For He Himself has said, "I will never leave you nor forsake you."
>
> — HEBREWS 13:5

I'm sure you've heard this truth. There are poems, greeting cards, and sermons based on this Scripture. But have you truly *heard* it? Has it traveled that distance from your head to your heart?

Your past experiences may interfere with your ability to absorb this truth. Unfortunately, people aren't as consistent as God. You may have been abandoned by a father, friend, or husband. But God will never leave you. As a born-again believer, you can always count on His presence.

God's Holy Spirit is with you right now as you're reading this. He stays with you day and night. And He's invited you to cast all your cares on Him. He loves you, dear sister. Pray and tell Him what you're thinking and how you're feeling. You can rely on Him.

HEART WORK

1. Most, if not all, of us have been left or forsaken at some point in our lives. Briefly journal about a time when that happened to you (e.g., a friend turned away from you or your father left when you were young).

2. Write out a prayer asking God to help you remember that, unlike people, He always keeps His promises. Ask Him to help you keep your past experiences from interfering with your ability to trust Him.

PRAYER CORNER

Abba, Father, we praise You for Your presence in our lives. Thank You for Your promise that You will never leave or forsake us. It's amazing that You are with us every moment of every day. Please help us to internalize and remember this promise. In Jesus' name, amen.

Day 2

 Fear not, for I am with you; be not dismayed, for I am your God. I will strengthen you, yes, I will help you, I will uphold you with My righteous right hand.

— ISAIAH 41:10

When you're confused, your thoughts may spiral as you focus on the problem instead of on your amazing God. It's easy to forget that God's Holy Spirit is with you because you don't always tangibly feel His presence. But God has promised that He's there—every second of every day.

You may have little or no control over a situation. But God does. He is sovereign; He is in control of everything. Nothing touches your life that He didn't allow. And God is with you, ready to strengthen and help you. That's why being conscious of God's presence is a game-changer: He'll help you navigate through every circumstance. You can rely on Him. He'll get you through it.

HEART WORK

1. How does remembering that God is with you change how you will approach today's challenges?

2. Write out Psalm 28:7. Memorize it and meditate on it. How has God helped you before when you trusted in Him?

PRAYER CORNER

Abba, Father, You are an awesome God. You are stronger than we could ever fully understand. You're the One who spoke the universe into existence. Please help us to trust You with everything we're going through today — to rest in the truth that You've revealed to us. In Jesus' name, amen.

"Never let the presence of a storm cause you to doubt the presence of God."

– Craig Groeschel[1]

Day 3

> I can never escape from Your Spirit! I can never get away from Your presence! If I go up to heaven, You are there; if I go down to the grave, You are there. If I ride the wings of the morning, if I dwell by the farthest oceans, even there Your hand will guide me, and Your strength will support me.
>
> — PSALM 139:7–10 (NLT)

You are not alone. It may *feel* like you are. Your emotions are real, but sometimes they lie. The truth is: No matter where you are or what's going on in your life, God is always with you. No ands, ifs, or buts. What matters is not how you feel but what God's Word says.

You may feel isolated—physically or emotionally. It may seem like no one knows what you're going through. But that isn't true. God understands your thoughts (Psalm 139:1–2). Bring everything to Him. He'll guide you and support you with His strength.

HEART WORK

1. Have you ever felt alone—even when you're surrounded by coworkers, family, or people at church? The next time that happens, what can you do to remind yourself that God is with you?

2. Write out 2 Corinthians 10:4–5. When you catch yourself thinking that you're alone or that no one understands you, how can you take that thought captive and make it obedient to Christ (i.e., how can you replace the lie with the truth)?

PRAYER CORNER

Abba, Father, it's awesome how You not only know our thoughts but understand them as well. Thank You for always being with us and caring for us. Please help us to remember Your presence so we will turn to You first with all our cares. In Jesus' name, amen.

Day 4

> In God (I will praise His word), in God I have put my trust; I will not fear.
>
> — PSALM 56:4

When something unexpected happens, what (or who) do you trust *first*? Do you call a friend before you pray? Do you cling to a statue of a saint or an angel? Is God an afterthought?

Don't put your trust in anything before Him. God created everything. Trusting in creation instead of *the* Creator results in idol worship. The universe can't help you. A statue of an angel can't see or hear you. A crystal won't empower you.

Go to God first—the One, true, all-powerful, sovereign God who is with you. He is all you need. Trust in the One who sees, hears, and is there by your side. Turn to Him today, and He will guide and strengthen you. He's your hope and your help.

HEART WORK

1. Write out Psalm 135:16–18. What do those verses tell you about idols?

2. Do you have anything or anyone in your life that you turn to for help or solace *before* going to God? Journal about it. Then ask God for forgiveness for going to those things first.

PRAYER CORNER

Abba, Father, please forgive us for going to people or other things before going to You. Please help us to remember that You are the One we should trust in and go to first, every time. You are the source of our strength. There is no one and nothing more powerful or able to help us than You. Thank You for caring for us. In Jesus' name, amen.

"The light of God's presence in our lives is a purifying flame that will draw us near to Him."

– Billy Graham[2]

Day 5

> Jesus answered and said to him, "If anyone loves Me, he will keep My word; and My Father will love him, and We will come to him and make Our home with him."

— JOHN 14:23

Today is another day filled with God's faithfulness. He didn't sneak out the back door while you were sleeping. As a born-again believer, He's made His home with you. And He'll be with you every moment as you go through your day.

Do you need someone to listen? Talk to Him, and He'll hear your prayers. Strength? Ask Him, and He'll strengthen you. Wisdom? He's promised to give it to you in abundance. God will fulfill His promise to be with you. Take a few minutes to thank Him for His presence in your life.

HEART WORK

1. Journal about how God saved you. What was your life like before you were born again? How has it been different since you came to Him?

2. Play your favorite worship song and sing it to God.

PRAYER CORNER

Abba, Father, it's hard for us to fully comprehend how amazing it is that the Almighty God is with us all the time. We praise You for how personal each of our relationships is with You. Please help us to know this with our hearts so we'll continually be in awe of You. In Jesus' name, amen.

Day 6

> " You will keep in perfect peace all who trust in You, all
> whose thoughts are fixed on You.

— ISAIAH 26:3 (NLT)

Who is with you? The one, true God is. The One who:

- Stretches out the heavens like a curtain (Isaiah 40:22).
- Measures the waters in the hollow of His hand
  (Isaiah 40:12).
- Calls all the stars by name (Isaiah 40:26 NLT).

Meditate on the truth that the One who is big enough and mighty enough to do these things will be with you throughout your day. If God can ensure that not one star is missing (Isaiah 40:26 NLT), He is able to help you. By keeping your thoughts fixed on Him, you'll be in perfect peace all day long.

HEART WORK

1. Write our Isaiah 40:26. How does it make you feel to know that your Creator is strong enough to ensure that all His creation is accounted for?

2. List seven attributes of God (e.g., He is omniscient, which means He knows everything). Spend at least five minutes thinking about the attributes you listed. Praise God for who He is.

PRAYER CORNER

Abba, Father, You are the great God who created the universe — the One who is bigger and more powerful than His creation. The things You have done keep us in awe of You as we meditate on them. It's amazing how much You care for us. Thank You for loving us. In Jesus' name, amen.

"If God is with you, so is His power. There is power in God's presence."

– Jackie Hill Perry[3]

Day 7

> Be anxious for nothing, but in everything by prayer and supplication, with thanksgiving, let your requests be made known to God; and the peace of God, which surpasses all understanding, will guard your hearts and minds through Christ Jesus.
>
> — PHILIPPIANS 4:6–7

Life is hard. A new (or continuing) difficulty may seem impossible to solve. Whatever it is, you can talk to God about it. He's right there with you, ready to listen. And He's given you a way to replace your worry with His supernatural peace that surpasses all understanding.

Pray. Come to God with all your requests. Lift them up to the One who can help you. Then thank Him for listening. Remember all the ways He's helped you in the past. Praise Him for His faithfulness. Finish by meditating on how awesome and amazing He is. Before you know it, you'll feel His peace—the peace that only He can give.

HEART WORK

1. Make a list of ten ways that God has provided for you in the past month.

2. Did you wake up this morning filled with anxiety? Write out a prayer telling God the things you are worried about and ask God for His strength to sustain you. End your prayer with gratitude for how God has provided for you and praise for who He is.

PRAYER CORNER

Abba, Father, thank You for this amazing promise and for giving us a way to replace our anxious thoughts with Your supernatural peace. When we're anxious, please remind us to come to You with everything. Please prompt us with Your Holy Spirit. In Jesus' name, amen.

Day 8

> If anyone serves Me, let him follow Me; and where I am, there My servant will be also. If anyone serves Me, him My Father will honor.

— JOHN 12:26

When God asks you to do something, it can be scary to take the first step. Whether He wants you to serve Him by checking in on a friend, sending someone an encouraging text, or praying with a coworker, you may be worried about how the person will respond.

But when you step out in faith to serve God, you don't have to do it alone. God is with you. He will help you. He will give you strength, wisdom, and everything you need to be obedient to His calling. Trust Him. Even if you don't see the results of your step of faith, remember: success is measured by your obedience and not by any accolades from others.

HEART WORK

1. What is God calling you to do today? Write it down. Pray and ask God for His help. Thank Him for the opportunity to be His hands and feet.

2. At the end of the day, journal about your experience. What did you do? Were you obedient to God's calling?

PRAYER CORNER

Abba, Father, thank You for letting us partner with You to do Your work. Help us to be sensitive to the leading of Your Holy Spirit when You prompt us to step out in faith. Please remind us of Your presence in those moments. In Jesus' name, amen.

"A sense of the divine presence and indwelling bears the soul towards heaven as upon the wings of eagles."

– Charles Spurgeon[4]

Day 9

> And I give them eternal life, and they shall never perish; neither shall anyone snatch them out of My hand. My Father, who has given them to Me, is greater than all; and no one is able to snatch them out of My Father's hand. I and My Father are one.
>
> — JOHN 10:28–30

Sometimes it seems like the only constant in our lives is change. If you rely on the things of this world, you'll eventually be disappointed. Money comes and goes. People falter. And possessions wear out or get lost.

Yet, God never changes; He is constant. His promises are always true. You are safe in His hands. No one can take you from that place of safety. God is greater than anyone or anything that could try to separate you from Him. That truth will never change. You can trust Him with everything.

HEART WORK

1. How does it make you feel to know that you are safe in God's hands—that no matter what happens in this life, you will live with Him for eternity?

2. Write out Hebrews 13:8. What did you learn about Jesus? Praise Him for His constancy.

～◊～

PRAYER CORNER

Abba, Father, we thank You for Your promise that we are in Your powerful, loving hands. We praise You that no one can snatch us out of Your hands. You are stronger and greater than anyone or anything. Help us to remember who You are and this amazing promise. In Jesus' name, amen.

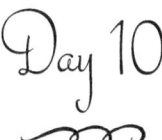

Day 10

 The LORD looks from heaven; He sees all the sons of men.

— PSALM 33:13

Do you sometimes feel like no one sees you? There may be days when it feels like you're invisible. When you walk into a room, maybe no one says hi or acknowledges your presence.

In those moments, remind yourself that you are not unseen. God sees you. Not only does He see you, but as His daughter, He is right there with you. You haven't gone unnoticed. Your Creator loves you and sees you every moment of every day.

Bask in God's love. Thank Him for His presence. Praise Him for His great care for you.

HEART WORK

1. Journal about a time when you felt invisible. How would that time have been different if you had reminded yourself that God sees you and loves you?

2. You're not the only one who sometimes feels unseen. List three things you could do the next time you go to church to make someone feel welcome (e.g., say hi to someone who is sitting alone and ask how you could pray for her).

PRAYER CORNER

Abba, Father, thank You for seeing us and caring for us. Please help us to remember that You are there: watching, loving, caring, helping. Your love and care are amazing. The One, true God loves us and never turns away. We praise You for who You are. In Jesus' name, amen.

"God is watching us, but He loves us so much that He can't take His eyes off us. We may lose sight of God, but He never loses sight of us."

– Greg Laurie[5]

Day 11

He who calls you is faithful, who also will do it.

— 1 THESSALONIANS 5:24

Are you a planner? If you are, it's easy to map out your goals and all the things you want to do. You may even have a to-do list of items you check off as you go through your day.

Being a planner isn't a bad thing. But have you asked God about His plans for your life? He has called you. And He has prepared days for you.

You were created in Christ Jesus for good works. Every day, God has something for you to do—something with eternal significance. Don't be afraid to ask Him. No matter what it is, God will be with you. He'll remain faithful as He works in and through you. He will be with you every step of the way, helping you to do whatever He's called you to do.

HEART WORK

1. Write out Ephesians 2:10. Pray and ask God to show you the good works He's prepared for you. Spend time in His Word, the Bible, each day, and listen for what He wants to reveal to you.

2. Examine yourself. Have you been following God's plan or yours? Pray and ask God. Then journal about what He shows you.

―∽∾―

PRAYER CORNER

Abba, Father, please show us the individual plans You have made for each of us. And please help us to yield our plans to Yours whenever Your plans are different from the ones we came up with on our own. Thank You for Your faithfulness — that we can count on Your guidance and help with all that You've called us to do. In Jesus' name, amen.

Day 12

 I am with you always, even to the end of the age.

— MATTHEW 28:20

Jesus said this to His disciples before He ascended into heaven. Maybe it was in response to what it tells us earlier in that chapter, "When they saw Him, they worshiped Him; but some doubted" (Matthew 28:17).

Did you wake up with doubts this morning? If so, Jesus wants you to know this truth. He is with you now. And He'll be with you later, too. That phrase, "to the end of the age," means for all eternity.

What an awesome promise from an amazing God! Praise Jesus for His promise. Let it sink deep into your mind until it makes its way to your heart. Meditate on the knowledge that Jesus is with you as you go through your day.

HEART WORK

1. Write out Ephesians 3:17–19. What did Paul want the Ephesians and all the saints to know?

2. Did you know that you're a saint? By virtue of being born again, you are. How does it make you feel to know how much Jesus loves you?

∽◠◠

PRAYER CORNER

Abba, Father, please help us to comprehend the extent of Your love for us. Let that fact sink deep into our minds so we'll meditate on it all throughout the day. And help us to internalize it so we'll know it with our hearts as well. In Jesus' name, amen.

"Only when we are captured by an overwhelming sense of awe and reverence in the presence of God, will we begin to worship God in spirit and in truth."

– Alistair Begg[6]

Day 13

> So be strong and courageous! Do not be afraid and do not panic before them. For the LORD your God will personally go ahead of you. He will neither fail you nor abandon you.
>
> — DEUTERONOMY 31:6 (NLT)

Trials always seem to sneak up on you, don't they? In an instant, the trajectory of your life changes. You don't know how you'll get through it, where it's going, or when it will end. The uncertainty may cause you to panic.

Yet, the One who is with you knows the beginning from the end. Your trial didn't surprise God. Don't be afraid. Not only will *the* Almighty God walk with you through the trial, but He'll personally go ahead of you. He won't fail you. And He won't abandon you. You can trust Him.

HEART WORK

1. Write out Psalm 23:4. What did the psalmist say he didn't need to fear? Why?

2. A shepherd used a rod and a staff when caring for his sheep. The rod was used to fight off predators, and the staff had a crook on one end to pull the sheep out of danger. How do these tools in Jesus'—the Good Shepherd's—hands comfort you?

PRAYER CORNER

Abba, Father, we praise You for being a personal God who goes ahead of us — the One who never fails or abandons us. Please help us to remember this truth. Increase our faith so we're not afraid. You are worthy of all our trust. In Jesus' name, amen.

Day 14

 How long, O LORD? Will You forget me forever?
How long will You hide Your face from me?

— PSALM 13:1

In this psalm, David felt like God had forgotten about him. If you've read about David in the Bible, you know that's not true. God had a plan for David's life, and He used the trials to prepare him for it.

Although David was at a low point, notice what he did: he prayed. He told God what he was thinking. And as he prayed, God did a work in his heart. By the end of the psalm, David recognized that God had "dealt bountifully" with him and decided that he would sing to God because of it (Psalm 13:6).

If you woke up this morning feeling forgotten, remind yourself of the truth. God hasn't forgotten you. Like David, pray. Tell God how you're feeling. Be honest with Him. As you do, God will do a work in your heart, too, reminding you of His faithfulness.

HEART WORK

1. Have you asked God for something but are still waiting for an answer? Maybe you've been praying for a loved one's salvation for years, and it seems like nothing has changed. Write out your concerns and relinquish them to God.

2. Write out Psalm 27:14. Pray through those words and personalize them in your prayer.

PRAYER CORNER

Abba, Father, please help us to remember that when we feel like You have forgotten us, You haven't. We praise You for always working everything together for good — even when we can't see it. In Jesus' name, amen.

"God's presence is not the same as the feeling of God's presence and He may be doing most for us when we think He is doing least."

– C.S. Lewis[7]

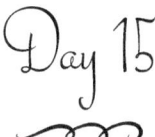

Day 15

 Therefore, humble yourselves under the mighty hand of God, that He may exalt you in due time, casting all your care upon Him, for He cares for you.

—1 PETER 5:6–7

Pride can keep you from asking for help. But aspiring to be self-sufficient is a man-made doctrine. The saying, "God helps those who help themselves," isn't in the Bible. Instead, God wants you to humble yourself under His mighty hand and cast all your care on Him. Why? Because He cares about you.

What is heavy on your heart today? You don't have to handle it alone. Recognize your need for God's help. He's right there with you. He won't make you, but He wants you to come to Him. He loves you. Pray and talk to God about what's going on in your life. Tell Him what makes you anxious. He will hear you. And He will strengthen you as you go through your day.

HEART WORK

1. We don't pray enough. The Bible tells us to "pray without ceasing" (1 Thessalonians 5:17). That's because communicating with God about everything as we go through our day is vital. He's our lifeline. List four ways you can remind yourself to pray throughout your day.

2. Write out a prayer praising God for His constant presence in your life. Without it, you wouldn't be able to go to Him whenever you wanted.

PRAYER CORNER

Abba, Father, You are amazing! You are the Almighty God who created the heavens, the earth and everything on it, the seas and all that is in them. Yet, You're right there with us every moment of every day. You make time for us and help us. Thank You for Your presence in our lives. Please help us to remember this awesome truth as we go through the day. In Jesus' name, amen.

Day 16

 Be still, and know that I am God; I will be exalted among the nations, I will be exalted in the earth!

— PSALM 46:10

This is a command, not a request. God says to be still before Him. As you're still, remember who He is. After all, He is the One, true God. There is no other. He's more important than anyone or anything. He's the Creator, and you are His creation.

Yet, in this busy world, it's easy to forget to do that. Let's be real: there are days when we forget about God altogether. Our daily plans often don't include allocating time to be still before Him, thinking about how amazing He is. We get self-focused, making it seem like the world revolves around us.

Make today different. Remind yourself to focus on God. Set aside time to be still before Him. Be in awe that the Creator of the universe has promised to be with you and praise Him for who He is.

HEART WORK

1. Take five minutes to be still before God. During that time, think about how amazing He is as the Creator of the universe and as your Creator. Meditate on His power and might.

2. Journal about the time you spent being still before God. How do you feel after focusing on His strength, knowing He is with you and loves you? Did He speak to you while you were focused on Him?

PRAYER CORNER

Abba, Father, You are God alone. No one and nothing is before You. You are the sovereign, Almighty God — our Creator and Savior. We praise You for who You are. Please help us to love You with all that we are and everything You've blessed us with. You deserve all the glory. In Jesus' name, amen.

"God didn't say, 'Be still and feel that I am God,' He said, 'Be still and know.'"

– Louie Giglio[8]

Day 17

> "Do not be afraid of their faces, for I am with you to deliver you," says the LORD.

— JEREMIAH 1:8

How would your day be different if you remembered that God is with you?

- Would it change the way you speak?
- Would you be bold enough to tell someone about Jesus?
- Would you refrain from doing something that you wouldn't want to do in His presence?

Remember: you are the temple of God, and His Spirit dwells in you (1 Corinthians 3:16). Meditate on the fact that God is with you. Don't be afraid of their faces. Live differently because of God's presence.

HEART WORK

1. Picture the faces of those who make you afraid (e.g., someone you haven't told you're a Christian because you don't know how she'll react). Now, picture God's presence in your mind, as if He were physically sitting or standing next to you. List the things you would do if you trusted that God is with you.

2. Write our Hebrews 12:2. Where should your eyes be? How can you keep your eyes on Him?

PRAYER CORNER

Abba, Father, thank You for the numerous reminders in Your Word that You are with us, that You're right there to help and comfort us. Please help us to remember this truth so we'll live like You're with us — because You are. In Jesus' name, amen.

Day 18

> If any of you lacks wisdom, let him ask of God, who gives to all liberally and without reproach, and it will be given to him.

— JAMES 1:5

God is full of wisdom—the right application of knowledge. God's wisdom is more valuable than gold (Proverbs 16:16). And He has promised to give it to you liberally and without reproach when you ask for it. That means He'll give it to you in abundance and He won't chastise you for asking.

As you make decisions today, turn to the One who is right there with you. When you do, ask Him for wisdom in faith, without doubting (James 1:6). Believe what He's said. Trust that He'll follow through. Whether your decision is big or small, God will show you what to do. There's no one better to go to than the One who knows all things.

HEART WORK

1. Journal about a decision you need to make today. Then pray over that decision, asking God for His wisdom in making it.

2. Write James 1:5 on an index card. Carry it around with you. Use it as a tool to help you memorize this truth. Pull it out and look at it as you go through your day.

PRAYER CORNER

Abba, Father, thank You for sharing Your wisdom with us. We praise You that You know exactly what we should do, ask, or say in every situation — that You can see the beginning from the end and how one action will affect everything else. Please help us to turn to You first in every situation. In Jesus' name, amen.

"We may ignore, but we can nowhere evade the presence of God. The world is crowded with Him. He walks everywhere incognito."

– C. S. Lewis[9]

Day 19

> "Look!" he answered, "I see four men loose, walking in the midst of the fire; and they are not hurt, and the form of the fourth is like the Son of God."

— DANIEL 3:25

When Shadrach, Meshach, and Abed-Nego refused to bow down and worship the gold image that King Nebuchadnezzar set up, they knew the consequences—being cast into a burning fiery furnace (Daniel 3:11). Yet, they trusted that God would deliver them (Daniel 3:17). And God did. But He didn't take them *out of* the trial. Instead, He walked with them *through* it.

If you're in a trial today, remember that. God may not deliver you from the trial, but He will walk with you through it, protecting you and strengthening you. No matter how hot it gets, He'll stay with you, every step of the way.

HEART WORK

1. If you're in a trial, journal about your concerns and surrender them to God.

2. Think back on a past trial. List the ways God helped you through it. If you're having trouble seeing God's hand, pray and ask Him to show you. Praise God for His faithfulness.

PRAYER CORNER

Abba, Father, thank You for all the ways You help us — for walking with us through every trial that comes our way. Please help us to always turn to You, no matter what we're going through. In Jesus' name, amen.

Day 20

> In Your presence is fullness of joy; at Your right hand
> are pleasures forevermore.

— PSALM 16:11

Slow down today and remind yourself of God's presence. Set a
reminder on your phone, put a sticky note on your desk, or do whatever will help you remember that God is with you. When you see
your reminder:

- Take a few minutes to think about who God is.
- Thank God for His presence in your life.
- Praise God for who He is and all He has done.
- Put on your favorite worship song and sing it to God.

There is nothing like being in God's presence. Take time to experience it and the joy that comes when you're consciously in it.

HEART WORK

1. Write out Psalm 84:10. Where did the psalmist prefer to be?

2. Think about a time when you enjoyed God's presence. Journal about it. How did it make you feel?

PRAYER CORNER

Abba, Father, You are our joy. Please help us to remember that there is nothing comparable to being in Your presence, surrounded by Your love. Help us to regularly make time to sit at Your feet, meditating on who You are and praising You. In Jesus' name, amen.

"Nothing in or of this world measures up to the simple pleasure of experiencing the presence of God."

– Aiden Wilson Tozer[10]

Day 21

> Remember the former things of old, for I am God, and there is no other; I am God, and there is none like Me, declaring the end from the beginning, and from ancient times things that are not yet done . . . .
>
> — ISAIAH 46:9–10

God wants you to remember all He has done. You can read about those things in the Bible. He's personally worked in and through your life, too. He is the Creator—the One who has performed miracles.

When you remember who God is and what He has done, your faith is built up. And when your faith is strong, it helps you to trust the One who is worthy of your trust. You don't know what the day holds. But God does. He knows everything you'll experience, what you'll need, and when you will need it. And the One who has declared the beginning from the end is with you.

HEART WORK

1. Think of at least five ways God helped His people, the Israelites, and journal about them (e.g., He parted the Red Sea so they could pass through on dry ground (Exodus 14:22)).

2. Remember at least five ways God has helped you. Write them down. Praise God for His faithfulness in your life.

PRAYER CORNER

Abba, Father, please help us to learn about and then remember all of the amazing things You have done. And help us to remember the ways You've been faithful in our lives. You have done great things — both then and now. We praise You for Your faithfulness. Thank You for loving and caring for us. In Jesus' name, amen.

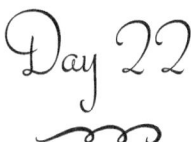

Day 22

> And what agreement has the temple of God with idols? For you are the temple of the living God. As God has said: "I will dwell in them and walk among them. I will be their God, and they shall be My people."
>
> — 2 CORINTHIANS 6:16

If you've been born again, you are the temple of the living God, and He dwells in you. This is God's truth. It's not about how you felt this morning when you woke up. Whether you started your day with a smile on your face or a heavy heart, God's promise remains true: He will not abandon you.

If you're sad, cry out to Him. If you are happy, sing a song praising Him. Pray and tell God what you're thinking and how you're feeling. Keep your focus on your God. You belong to Him.

HEART WORK

1. Write out Psalm 139:23–24. Depending on the version, verse 24 may use the English words *wicked, grievous,* or *hurtful* for the Hebrew word *oseb*, which means idol— anything you've been prioritizing before God. The New Living Translation says, "Point out anything in me that *offends* You . . . ." Pray through those verses and ask God to show you if there is anything you've been prioritizing before Him.

2. After you pray through Psalm 139:23–24, sit still before God. Journal about what God reveals to you about your heart.

PRAYER CORNER

Abba, Father, it's hard to grasp the fact that You dwell in us. Please help us to fully understand this truth: that each of us becomes Your temple the moment we're born again. Equip us to live like we're Your temple — to honor You by making You preeminent in our lives. We thank You for Your amazing plan. In Jesus' name, amen.

"Don't equate the presence of God with a good mood or a pleasant temperament. God is near whether you are happy or not."

— Max Lucado[11]

Day 23

> Have I not commanded you? Be strong and of good courage; do not be afraid, nor be dismayed, for the LORD your God is with you wherever you go.
>
> — JOSHUA 1:9

God gave this promise to Joshua as Joshua stepped into his new role as the leader of the nation of Israel. You may not be leading a nation today. Yet, you're probably a leader in some respect—whether you supervise people at work, have children in your care, teach Sunday school, or have friends who value your opinion.

The promise God gave to Joshua applies to you, as well, because God's character and nature do not change. You don't need to be afraid of whatever you're called to do today because God is with you. He will give you strength and all the wisdom you need when you ask Him. The One who called you is able to help you.

HEART WORK

1. Think about your life and write down anyone you lead. Then journal a prayer asking God to give you strength and courage to be a godly influence in their lives.

2. This wasn't the first time God told Joshua to be strong and of good courage. Read Joshua 1:6–7. Why do you think God repeated this exhortation to Joshua three times?

PRAYER CORNER

Abba, Father, please help us to keep our minds fixed on Your promise that You will be with us wherever we go. Help us to internalize the truth that You are right there, strengthening us and giving us courage every step of the way. Thank You for being with us. In Jesus' name, amen.

Day 24

 If we are faithless, He remains faithful; He cannot deny Himself.

— 2 TIMOTHY 2:13

Let's face it. People are flawed (including you). No one is perfect. Sometimes they will let you down.

But God is . . . well, God. He is perfect. He will never fail you. His promise to be with you will never change. He is always true; He always keeps His promises.

And this truth isn't contingent on anything you can do. Even when you are faithless, God cannot deny who He is. If you have a bad day, His promise remains true. So, when life feels scary and unpredictable, remember this truth. You can always count on God to be there with you. Wherever you are and whatever your circumstances, He remains faithful.

HEART WORK

1. Write out 1 Samuel 7:12. List a milestone in your life that God helped you to reach. Like Samuel, set up an Ebenezer stone to remind you of God's faithfulness in your life.

2. Journal a prayer praising God for His faithfulness.

PRAYER CORNER

Abba, Father, what an amazing promise this is! We thank You that Your very nature is to remain faithful even when we aren't. You are so good to us. Help us to meditate on how awesome You are. In Jesus' name, amen.

"We (Christians) are always in the presence of God. There is never a non-sacred moment! His presence never diminishes. Our awareness of His presence may falter, but the reality of His presence never changes."

– Max Lucado[12]

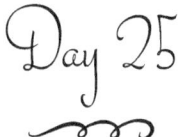

Day 25

Say to those with fearful hearts, "Be strong, and do not fear, for your God is coming to destroy your enemies. He is coming to save you."

— ISAIAH 35:4 (NLT)

God does His work in so many ways. He could do His work without us. Yet, one way He works is through us—when we're willing to step out in faith.

You are called, dear sister, to encourage the people God has placed in your life. Some of them have fearful hearts. They need to be reminded that God will save them.

If you see someone with a fearful heart, don't hesitate to be the hands and feet of Jesus. Take time to encourage her. Tell her that God is the One who will save her from her enemies. Pray with her. Help her to focus on the One who can truly help.

HEART WORK

1. Read 1 Samuel 30:6. What did David do when he was greatly distressed? If you're troubled, you can do the same. Strengthen yourself in the Lord your God by spending time reading the Bible, singing along with your favorite worship music, listening to a sermon, and fellowshipping with other believers at your church.

2. Do you know someone who needs encouragement? Write down her name. Pray for her. Then text or call her and let her know that you're praying for her.

PRAYER CORNER

Abba, Father, thank You for doing Your work through us. Please help us to be sensitive to the leading of Your Holy Spirit so we will hear when You prompt us to encourage someone who has a fearful heart. Give us strength and the words we need to step into their lives and tell them about You — the source of their help. In Jesus' name, amen.

Day 26

❝ The LORD is far from the wicked, but He hears the prayer of the righteous.

— PROVERBS 15:29

You are righteous—not because of anything you have done—but based on the fact that Jesus died on the cross for your sins. When you accepted God's free gift of salvation, Jesus adorned you with His robe of righteousness.

Now, in Christ Jesus, God sees Jesus' righteousness when He looks at you. And He hears your prayers because of it. Every time you talk to Him, He is listening. If you're worried, pray. If you need to make a decision, pray. Intercede for your family. Take everything to the One who can help you. Nothing is too big or too small. Acknowledge His presence and rely on Him.

HEART WORK

1. Read Isaiah 61:10. What does that verse say God has done for you?

2. Write out 2 Corinthians 5:21. What did God do so we could become righteous?

~~

PRAYER CORNER

Abba, Father, it's amazing that You consider us righteous because of what Your Son, Jesus, has done for us. Thank You for hearing our prayers. Please help us to remember to come to You first with everything we need. In Jesus' name, amen.

"If you feel far from God right now, guess who moved? You're only a decision away from reconnecting."

– Anne Graham Lotz[13]

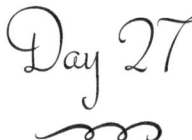

Day 27

 Call to Me, and I will answer you, and show you great and mighty things, which you do not know.

— JEREMIAH 33:3

Some have jokingly referred to Jeremiah 33:3 as God's phone number. Why? That verse is a great reminder of how to reach God.

It's simple: call to Him. He's not distant. All you have to do is start talking, and He will hear you. Take Him up on His invitation to call to Him.

When you do, He'll answer. And most of the time, He'll answer you through His Word, the Bible. He wants to show you great and mighty things. Cry out to Him today. Then open up your Bible and listen to Him speak to you.

HEART WORK

1. Write out Hebrews 1:1–2. Who has God spoken through?

2. Journal about how God has been speaking to you through His Word, the Bible.

PRAYER CORNER

Abba, Father, thank You for making Yourself available to us. It's awesome that You — the One, true God — cares about us so much that You invite us to call out to You. Thank You for speaking to us through the prophets and Your Son, Jesus, so we can know great and mighty things. You are amazing! In Jesus' name, amen.

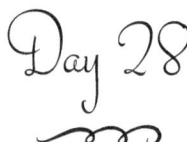

Day 28

> Fear not, for I have redeemed you; I have called you by
> your name; you are Mine. When you pass through the
> waters, I will be with you; and through the rivers, they
> shall not overflow you. When you walk through the
> fire, you shall not be burned, nor shall the flame
> scorch you.

— ISAIAH 43:1–2

Your creator calls you by name. He's redeemed you, and you belong to Him. You don't need to be afraid. He is with you.

It may *feel* like the waters of your trial are about to wash over your head. It may *seem* like the fire is heating up to consume you. But that isn't true. God has promised that the waters won't overflow you; you won't get burned or scorched. Stop trying to control the situation. Ask God to increase your faith and rely on Him. Trust Him with the outcome.

HEART WORK

1. Write out Romans 8:28–29. How many things is God working together for good? Meditate on the promise God has made to you in those verses.

2. For what purpose does God allow trials in your life? (Hint: Look at Romans 8:29.) Think about a trial you've gone through in the past. Journal about the differences you can see in your life since that trial.

PRAYER CORNER

Abba, Father, thank You for using our circumstances to conform us into the image of Your Son, Jesus. Help us to remember that our trials have a purpose. We want to be more like Jesus. Remind us to rely on You — to come to You for strength — the One who is with us through our trials. In Jesus' name, amen.

"We may be confident in this: that in the pain of our suffering is the presence of a faithful God."

– Alistair Begg[14]

Day 29

> " And I will pray the Father, and He will give you another Helper, that He may abide with you forever— the Spirit of truth, whom the world cannot receive, because it neither sees Him nor knows Him; but you know Him, for He dwells with you and will be in you.
>
> — JOHN 14:16–17

The Helper that Jesus promises in these verses is the Holy Spirit. As God's daughter, the Spirit dwells with you. And He doesn't abide with you for a short time or part-time. Instead, He stays with you forever, dear sister.

Not only that, but the same Spirit that raised Jesus from the dead is the One who lives in you (Romans 8:11). You don't have to wonder whether you'll have enough strength to face today. Whatever challenges lie ahead, the Helper will be there to supply all that you need to get you through them and glorify God along the way.

HEART WORK

1. Write out Galatians 5:22–23. Journal about a way that you've seen the fruit of the Spirit manifested in your life.

2. Read John 15:5. Are you lacking fruit? Pray and ask God to show you what you're lacking. Write down what He reveals. Then pray for Him to develop it in your life as you abide in Him.

∿

PRAYER CORNER

Abba, Father, we praise You for the presence of Your Holy Spirit in our lives. It inspires awe in us that the same One who raised Jesus from the dead lives in us. Thank You for loving us so much that You are always there to help us with everything we need. You are so good to us. In Jesus' name, amen.

Day 30

> He who dwells in the secret place of the Most High shall abide under the shadow of the Almighty.

— PSALM 91:1

As a born-again believer, God has made His home with you (John 14:23). It may seem counterintuitive at first, but you can remain close to God or move away from Him. You have a choice about where you will stay.

If you move away from Him, you'll be filled with your own ways (Proverbs 14:14). But as you enter into praise and worship, you'll be under the covering of the Most High—a place of safety and contentment. Dear sister, as we close out this devotional, I urge you to abide under the shadow of the Almighty. There's no better place you can be.

HEART WORK

1. Journal about the ways you can praise and worship God all throughout your day (e.g., sing to Him along with your favorite worship song in the car or read the Bible during a work break).

2. Write out Psalm 62:7. Meditate on the truth that your refuge is in God.

PRAYER CORNER

Abba, Father, You are the Most High — the Almighty God. We praise You for protecting us under Your shadow when we stay close to You. Please help us to stay put in Your presence all throughout our days. You are worthy of constant praise! In Jesus' name, amen.

"True and absolute freedom is only found in the presence of God."

– Aiden Wilson Tozer[15]

Notes

[1] Craig Groeschel (@craiggroeschel), "Never let the presence of a storm cause you to doubt the presence of God," X, July 22, 2016, 7:45 a.m., https://x.com/craiggroeschel/status/756485376974397440.

[2] Billy Graham Quotable Quote, Goodreads, accessed August 14, 2025, https://www.goodreads.com/quotes/7487494-the-light-of-god-s-presence-in-our-lives-is-a.

[3] Jackie Hill Perry (@jackiehillperry), "If God is with you, so is His power. There is power in God's presence," Instagram, March 24, 2023, https://www.instagram.com/p/CqLDirfA9P6/?hl=en-gb.

[4] Charles Spurgeon Quotes, Goodreads, accessed August 14, 2025, https://www.goodreads.com/quotes/tag/charles-spurgeon#:~:text=especially%20the%20Puritanic%20writers%2C%20and%20expositions%20of%20the%20Bible.&text=A%20sense%20of%20the%20divine,upon%20the%20wings%20of%20eagles.

[5] Greg Laurie, "Keeping Us in View," Devotion (blog), Harvest, October 31, 2014, https://harvest.org/resources/devotion/keeping-us-in-view/.

[6] Alistair Begg, QuoteFancy, accessed August 14, 2025, https://quotefancy.com/alistair-begg-quotes.

[7] C.S. Lewis Quotable Quote, Goodreads, accessed August 14, 2025, https://www.goodreads.com/quotes/8722257-god-s-presence-is-not-the-same-as-the-feeling-of.

[8] Louie Giglio, "Best Quotes from Catalyst 15," *Lifeway Leadership*, accessed August 14, 2025, https://leadership.lifeway.com/2015/10/19/best-quotes-from-catalyst-15/.

[9] C.S. Lewis Quotable Quote, Goodreads, accessed August 14, 2025, https://www.goodreads.com/quotes/110487-we-may-ignore-but-we-can-nowhere-evade-the-presence.

[10] Aiden Wilson Tozer, QuoteFancy, accessed August 14, 2025, https://quotefancy.com/quote/1446690/Aiden-Wilson-Tozer-Nothing-in-or-of-this-world-measures-up-to-the-simple-pleasure-of.

[11] Max Lucado Quotable Quote, Goodreads, accessed August 14, 2025, https://www.goodreads.com/quotes/6472647-don-t-equate-the-presence-of-god-with-a-good-mood.

[12] Max Lucado Quotes, AZ Quotes, accessed August 14, 2025, https://www.azquotes.com/quote/857025.

[13] Anne Graham Lotz Quotable Quote, Goodreads, accessed August 14, 2025, https://www.goodreads.com/quotes/1178698-if-you-feel-far-from-god-right-now-guess-who.

[14] Alistair Begg (@AlistairBegg), "We may be confident in this: that in the pain of our suffering is the presence of a faithful God," X, November 20, 2020, 3:06 p.m., https://x.com/AlistairBegg/status/1329909006383656970.

[15] Aiden Wilson Tozer, QuoteFancy, accessed August 14, 2025, https://quotefancy.com/quote/1446591/Aiden-Wilson-Tozer-True-and-absolute-freedom-is-only-found-in-the-presence-of-God.

About the Author

Catherine McDaugale is an attorney-turned-author who wants to honor God with her writing. She loves to create stories that entertain and edify. In addition to novels, she writes nonfiction books and devotionals to teach others about the Christian faith and help them draw near to God. A new devotional is published every other week on her website: CatherineMcDaugale.com.

Also by Catherine McDaugale

NONFICTION

Ebenezer Stones (a Bible study about God's faithfulness)

Ebenezer Stones Study Guide

How to Teach Your Kids about God

FICTION

The Door: A Novel

www.ingramcontent.com/pod-product-compliance
Lightning Source LLC
Chambersburg PA
CBHW071518120626
46550CB00006B/2262